This Journal Belongs To:

Organize your thoughts, make lists,
out your desires, record your memories,
document your days or weeks or months,
catalog recipes, note books to read, list
flora and fauna discovered, keep track
of bright ideas and secret inventions.

Fill these pages with words or
pictures in any order you need.

Make it yours.

Nikki McClure

THINGS TO MAKE AND DO
A Journal

SASQUATCH BOOKS
SEATTLE

PLANS

GRAVITY

WISHES

WISHES

DREAMS

DREAMS

DREAMS

DREAMS

DREAMS

BUILD

BUILD

BUILD

BUILD

EXPLORE

EXPLORE

EXPLORE

LEARN

LEARN

LEARN

INCUBATE

LEARN

MAKE

MAKE

PROVIDE

MAKE

MAKE

GROW

GROW

ENCOURAGE

GROW

GIVE

INVEST

GIVE

TREASURE

FIND

FIND

FIND

Using an X-acto knife, a single sheet of paper, and the inspiration that surrounds her at her Olympia, Washington, home, Nikki McClure lovingly creates her intricate and beautiful paper cuts. Her work constructs a bold graphic language that translates the complex poetry of family, nature, and activism into endearing, positive, and disarmingly powerful images. Nikki makes a calendar every year as well as many books and pies.

www.nikkimcclure.com

Printed in China
Printed on recycled paper
Published by Sasquatch Books
Distributed by PGW/Perseus
15 14 13 12 11 10 09 08 9 8 7 6 5 4 3 2 1

Book design: Kate Basart/Union Pageworks
ISBN-10: 1-57061-564-0 ISBN-13: 978-1-57061-564-1
SASQUATCH BOOKS
119 South Main Street, Suite 400 | Seattle, WA 98104 206.467.4300
www.sasquatchbooks.com | custserv@sasquatchbooks.com